Imperfectly Perfect
Mental Health Is Real

Written By *Ruso*
Illustrated By *Gracena G.*

To order additional copies of this book, contact:
Xlibris
844-714-8691
www.Xlibris.com
Orders@Xlibris.com

Library of Congress Control Number: 2022916859
ISBN: Softcover   978-1-6698-4678-9
        Hardcover   978-1-6698-4677-2
        EBook   978-1-6698-4679-6

Library of Congress Control Number: 2022916859

Print information available on the last page

Rev. date: 10/14/2022

* Lauren Brents *

Having a combination of anxiety and pretty severe ADHD really blows.. The ADHD makes it to where my mind is literally never silent. Something is always being thought through or memories being replayed or even just random thoughts that I can't turn off. Always every second of the day... The thing that really blows is that if my anxiety gets triggered it kicks the hyper focus part of my ADHD into overdrive and that's the one thing I can only think about until the end of time meds help... but only so much....

* K. Shamar *

I was exhausted from everything in my life. My emotions were so heavy that I didn't have enough strength to carry them close to me like fresh tattoos on my skin. Depression and anxiety have attached themselves to me like magnets not wanting to depart from me. I've cried for so long that I no-longer have tears left. Overwhelming feelings I feel like I'm crying someone else's tears this has to be more than pain this has to be generational trauma and my own thoughts haunts me everyday and night no matter what I do nothing helps, I've prayed. Cried out. Nothing seems to help finally I let go turned myself into a facility for treatment learned some coping skills and found some true friends that I could talk to and now I'm on my way... seek help... I love you.....

* Isaiah Gaines *

I deal with PTSD and anxiety... what I find that helps me with my PTSD I stay away from people that are bad influencers I've been taking counseling for 9yrs it helps... and my anxiety I cope by listening to music and using my breathing exercises when I feel overwhelmed or I do something productive... to take my mind of things.. staying busy... meds and therapy helps...

It's okay not
to be okay

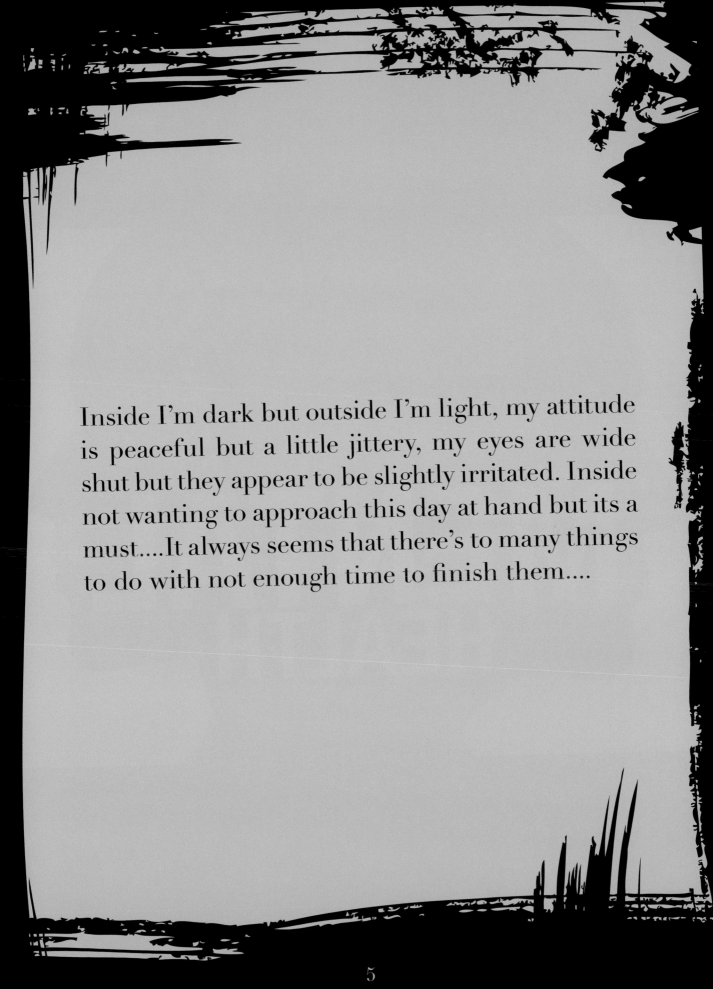

Inside I'm dark but outside I'm light, my attitude is peaceful but a little jittery, my eyes are wide shut but they appear to be slightly irritated. Inside not wanting to approach this day at hand but its a must....It always seems that there's to many things to do with not enough time to finish them....

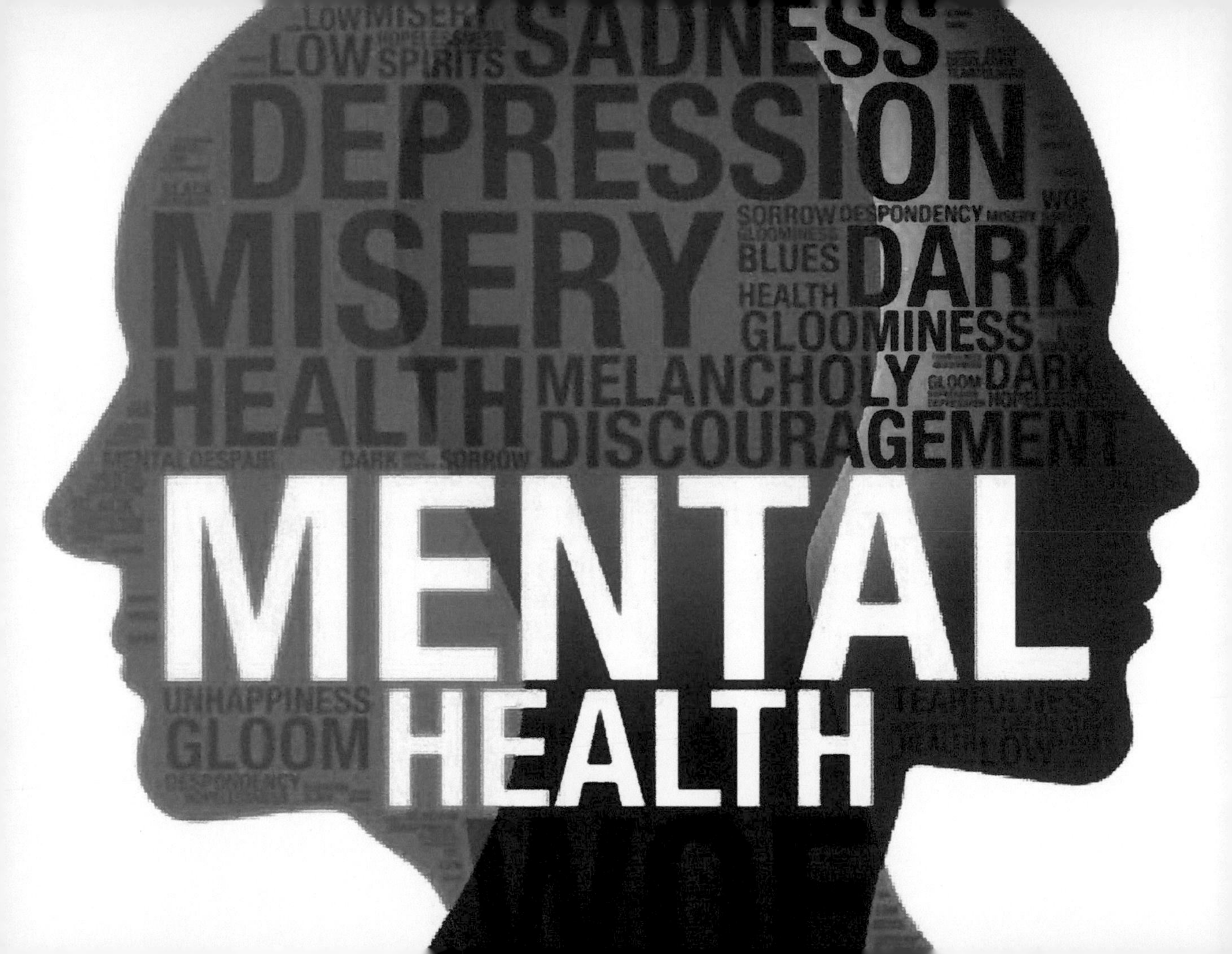
SADNESS
LOW
SPIRITS
DEPRESSION
MISERY
SORROW
DESPONDENCY
BLUES
DARK
HEALTH
GLOOMINESS
HEALTH
MELANCHOLY
GLOOM
DARK
DISCOURAGEMENT
DARK
SORROW
MENTAL
UNHAPPINESS
GLOOM
HEALTH

The day has just started and I'm crunched for time already. Guess this will be another day like the rest starting tasks and not being able to complete them. While trying to keep my feelings and emotions in tact. As I go out and try to conquer this world.... one second at a time.....

You Are Special

Ruso
Loves You

My inner-self always pushing me to keep going but my temple is beat down and has seen better days... I often ask why do I feel this way?

(Breath)
Why do I feel this way?
(Breath)
Why do I feel this way?

Well.....

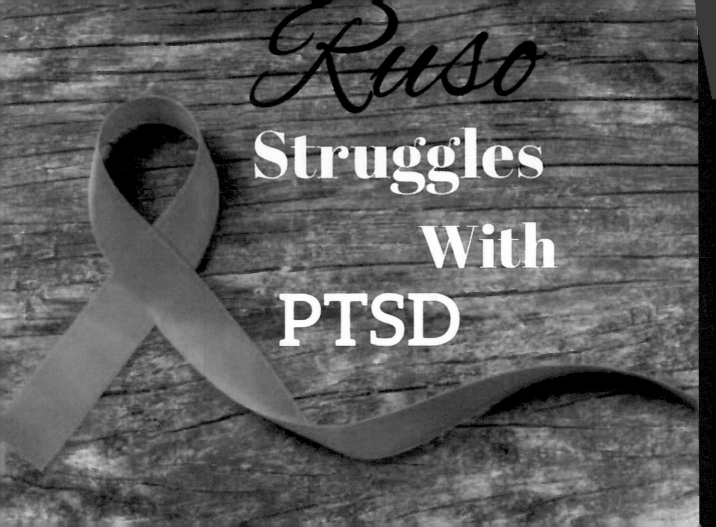

I was told my whole life that... black people and people of color don't have (mental health) problems but as I aged and learned that the myth I was taught as a youngster was absolutely false.. and very misleading. I wanted to change these teachings to the youth and raise awareness..... to all colors and genders of people.. Lets stop this ignorant way of teaching and save lives....

Mental Health

Your Not Alone

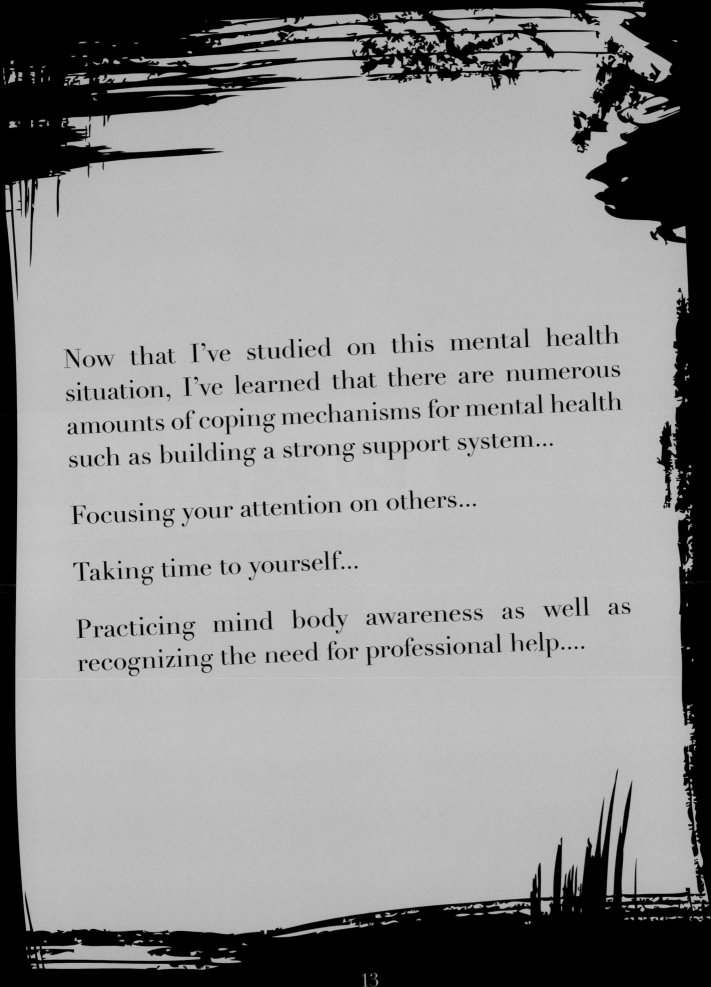

Now that I've studied on this mental health situation, I've learned that there are numerous amounts of coping mechanisms for mental health such as building a strong support system...

Focusing your attention on others...

Taking time to yourself...

Practicing mind body awareness as well as recognizing the need for professional help....

Remember it does not matter what you've been told your whole life professional help is great and it does wonders..

Therapy....

    Meds.....

        Or call the hotline 988

Again you must get help. Let your feeling run wild to someone who can untangle your thoughts and straighten out your path... of success....live your life to the fullest.. I realize that some of us have different mental issues like depression, bi-polarism, PTSD...anxiety etc...

Just know your not alone... never......

We love you.....

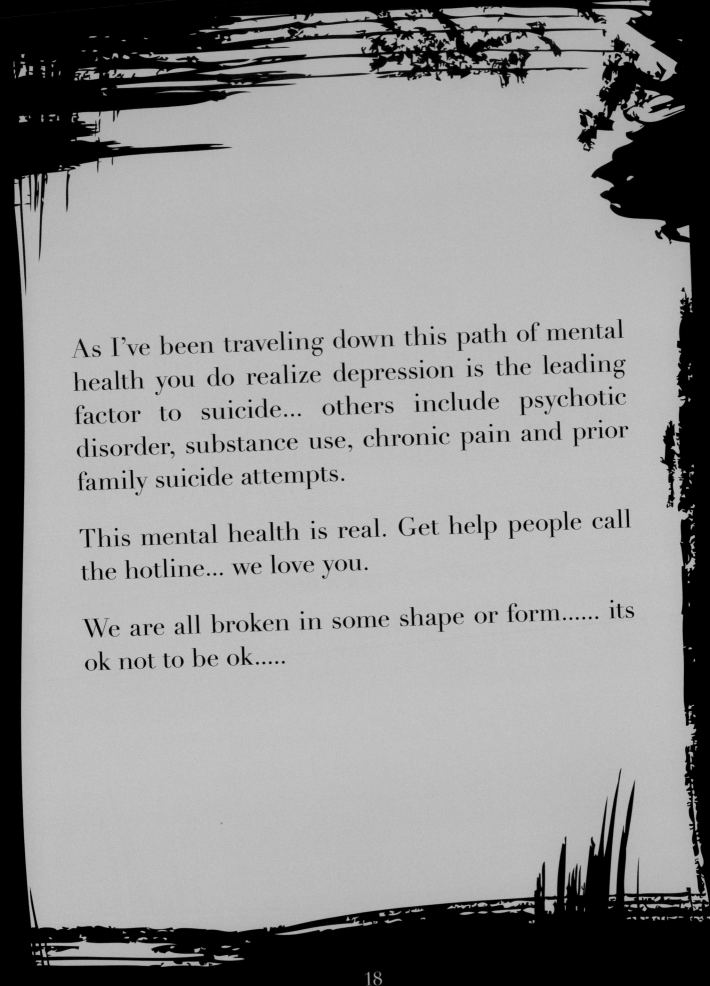

As I've been traveling down this path of mental health you do realize depression is the leading factor to suicide... others include psychotic disorder, substance use, chronic pain and prior family suicide attempts.

This mental health is real. Get help people call the hotline... we love you.

We are all broken in some shape or form...... its ok not to be ok.....

We all have someone in our family or a friend that is struggling with mental health and sees no way out. We must be their crutch...

Be their ear give them inspiration before its to late.. lets beat this mental health issue one Ruso- ism at a time. We must go on but before I proceed the National Suicide # is 988

Suicide is real... one more life is to many....

My people before I end, wanted to touch on some other disorders such as bipolar it was previously known as manic depression known as a mood disorder this one is characterized by periods of depression and elevated happiness that last for days to weeks.. but if the mood is elevated and severe its associated with psychosis basically a manic...we can write and talk for-ever but the real is it's here mental health ain't going no where and we must utilize our resources and get help. Call the hotline, seek community and get therapy... and stay woke.

Listen, listen, listen.

Mental Health...

Imperfectly Perfect....

* Dr. Ty *

Most people who live with mental illness have at some point been impugned for their illness. Name calling. Needing more prayer, and its a phase come in play. The stigma causes people to feel ashamed for something that is out of their control worst of all stigma thwarts people from seeking help.

All of us need to raise our voices against stigma everyday in every possible way we need to stand up to stigma no matter how you contribute to those struggling with mental health. You can make a difference simply by knowing that mental illness is not anyone's fault no matter what societal stigma says. You can make a change by being and living stigma FREE. National Suicide Hotline - 988 available 24/7

Ruso

Urban Author

Printed in the United States
by Baker & Taylor Publisher Services